DEPLOYMENT *journal* for SPOUSES

MEMORIES *and* MILESTONES

RACHEL ROBERTSON

Elva Resa ✳ Saint Paul

TO ALL WHO LOVE SOMEONE IN THE MILITARY

Thank you to those whose encouragement means so much:
Mom, Dad, David, Iztchel, Jane, Annie;
and to the team at Elva Resa, especially
Karen Pavlicin-Fragnito, Terri Barnes, and Brenda Harris;
and of course, Hanna and Abby.
~ Rachel

Deployment Journal for Spouses: Memories and Milestones
© 2008 (1st edition), © 2017 (2nd edition), © 2019 (3rd edition)
Rachel Robertson

ISBN: 978-1-934617-46-5

Printed in United States of America.

Elva Resa Publishing
8362 Tamarack Village, Suite 119-106
Saint Paul, Minnesota 55125

ElvaResa.com
MilitaryFamilyBooks.com

WHERE TO FIND IT

Your story is an important one.

When my husband received orders for his first deployment, my first thought was *I am not ready for this*. And even after we had been through several deployments, I could not predict how it would feel to have my husband leave again; how it would feel to keep a smile on my face for my daughter's sake, even when I hadn't heard from her dad in weeks; how it would feel to see our new baby on an ultrasound for the first time without my husband; how it would feel to be proud and afraid, worried and brave, all at the same time.

The idea of creating a deployment journal came to me when my husband deployed along with most of the Marines from our base, headed overseas into unknown dangers and limited communication opportunities. The stress and worry all around us felt heavy. I kept a journal during that deployment and others that followed. It was a place where I could let out my fear, anger, frustration, and worry. In those pages, I could be who I wanted to be and say what I wanted to say without worrying about anyone else. I could dream about life after the deployment; I could hash out what I felt about the evening—or 2 a.m.—news. My journal allowed me to let go of many of my feelings and be strong and positive for the rest of the day. Writing let me hurt and heal at the same time. And then, at the end of the deployment, I had a record of this pivotal time in my life.

Knowing the emotional benefits of journaling and how it helped me cope, I wrote a series of deployment journals: one for kids, one for spouses, and another for parents. Working on this edition of *Deployment Journal for Spouses* has taken me right back to how I felt in that time. Although years have gone by—global conflicts and deployment locations have changed—the need is the same, and journaling still provides the same comfort and benefits. Being a military spouse is not easy. It takes a special kind of strength.

My journal was so important to me, I wanted to help you have a similar experience during the deployment you're going through. Your story is an important one to tell and there's no one better to tell it than you.

How to use this journal

Being separated from someone you love is a challenge. No matter how much you rant and rave, worry, or cry, you can't change it. Thank goodness we have within us the power to turn a difficult situation into a meaningful and important life experience. This deployment is an opportunity to show what you are made of, especially to yourself. You can and will survive, and journaling can help.

Deployment Journal for Spouses is yours to use as you like and as you need throughout this experience. Write, doodle, draw, reflect, record, say things you can't say to anyone else, or make a keepsake for you and your spouse to look at when you are together again.

Specially-designed sections, with optional prompts, guide you through the deployment, from getting ready and saying goodbye, to readjusting after homecoming and looking forward. Together, these sections will help you reflect on your full experience and all you learn from it.

Emotional ups and downs are part of any deployment. Your feelings will likely change from day to day or moment to moment. Use journaling to help you recognize and process those feelings.

When you need inspiration or helpful tips for managing stress, family activities, or care packages, turn to the ideas and reminders pages.

Keep track of special memories and milestones at the back of the journal. These moments might include a meaningful letter or message from your spouse, children's accomplishments, personal goals you've met—any special moments you want to record.

Enjoy reflecting on your relationship with your service member. Communicate often. Track your milestones while apart. Together, you can make this adventure meaningful.

My very best wishes to you during this experience and my thanks for your courage. This is your deployment, too.

With thoughts of hope,

Rachel Robertson

A favorite photo of us

Our history

The first time we met ...

where we met ...   how old we were ...   who introduced us ...   what I was wearing ...   circumstances that brought us together ...   first words we said to each other ...

What we enjoy doing together ...

❧ walking in the park ❧ singing to the radio in the car ❧ a trip to the zoo ❧ taking photos
❧ karaoke ❧ watching old movies ❧ sitting next to each other in a diner booth ☙

Our favorites ...

>> restaurants >> movies >> books >> Friday night routines >> friends >> quotes >> heroes

>> Sunday morning plans >> road trips >> classic cars >> desserts >> holiday traditions

>> animals >> bands >> songs >> singers >> actors >> authors >> treats

Fondest memories together ...

Challenges we have faced together ...

RESIST THE

TEMPTATION

TO PONDER

what if

INSTEAD, LIVE

IN EACH

MOMENT OF

what is

Ways our love grows stronger ...

❧ *cheering for our favorite team* ❧ *flowers for no reason* ❧ *chasing critters out of the house* ❧ *laughing at an inside joke* ❧ *crying when it hurts* ❧ *laughing until we cry* ❧ *love notes on the bathroom mirror* ❧ *apologizing* ❧ *standing up for each other* ☙

15

Getting ready

We can grow stronger together even while we are apart ...

Deployment location: ♡

Home: ☆

How I heard the news ...

What I know about this deployment ...

What I want to know about this deployment ...

As I get ready for this deployment, I feel ...

Strong ❧ *Optimistic* ❧ *Frustrated* ❧ *Worried* ❧ *Loved* ❧ *Nervous* ❧ *Peaceful*

Grateful ❧ *Empty* ❧ *Joyous* ❧ *Determined* ❧ *Broken-hearted* ❧ *Exhausted*

Capable ❧ *Excited* ❧ *Hopeful* ❧ *Confused* ❧ *Angry* ❧ *Proud* ❧ *Blessed* ❧ *Relieved*

I can only be strong when I take care of myself. Ways I will make my physical and mental health a priority ...

Sometimes it's hard to ask for help, but I know I will need support during this deployment. I can count on these people:

NAME: CONTACT INFORMATION:

_____   _____

                                   _____

                                   _____

_____   _____

                                   _____

                                   _____

_____   _____

                                   _____

                                   _____

_____   _____

                                   _____

                                   _____

_____   _____

                                   _____

                                   _____

_____   _____

                                   _____

                                   _____

Ways we are preparing for our time apart ...

Saying goodbye

What I want to remember about our goodbye ...

the date we said goodbye ... people around us ... a special moment ... what the weather was like ... what I was wearing ... what we said to each another ...

I wish ... I hope ... I didn't expect ... I will ... One of the best ...

Now that we have said goodbye, I feel...

Afraid • Excited • Hopeful • Balanced • Furious • Proud • Blessed • Relieved

Creative • Optimistic • Sad • Smart • Loved • Worn-out • Overwhelmed

Teary • Exhausted • Healthy • Determined • Happy • Lonely • Grateful

Deployment

My goals during this deployment ...

DEPLOYMENT

I WANT TO

do more

THAN SIMPLY

endure

I WANT TO

LIVE WITH

purpose

I am grateful ...

I wonder ...

LETTERS *and* EMAILS

Written communication adds a new dimension to a relationship. It's good to send a note of some kind—postcard, letter, text, email, message in a bottle—every other day or so. Communications don't have to be long. Even a few words can create a connection.

I can:

~ Write handwritten notes.

~ Set a regular time for writing letters.

~ Know it's okay to write about the mundane.

~ Use our letters as a romantic way to get to know each other better.

~ Share feelings, not just facts about what's happening.

~ Answer questions and be clear when asking questions.

~ Keep a notebook to jot down what I want to share in my next letter.

~ Share stories from our life and confide dreams for our future.

~ Avoid writing when I'm angry or depressed. I'll journal those feelings first before putting them in a letter.

~ Save letters and emails in a special place as a keepsake.

~ Keep track of important letters, emails, and phone calls in the memories and milestones pages of this journal.

❧ *I wish we could have shared this moment together ...* ❧ *I am looking forward to ...*
❧ *I'm glad I had the opportunity to ...* ❧ *The best thing about today was ...* ❧

❧ *The hardest part of this deployment so far is ...* ❧ *My friends have helped me in this*
deployment by ... ❧ *Things that bring me joy ...* ❧ *It feels good to laugh ...* ☙

LOOK FOR

joy

IT IS THERE

ready

WHEN YOU ARE

❧ DEPLOYMENT ☙

Today, I feel ...

Playful → *Confident* → *Open-minded* → *Loving* → *Annoyed* → *Quirky* → *Bold*

Uncertain → *Eager* → *Vibrant* → *Jealous* → *Impatient* → *Lonely* → *Thankful*

→ *Surprised* → *Tired* → *Cheerful* → *Grouchy* → *Fed-up* → *Proud* → *Lucky* → *Rejuvenated*

DEPLOYMENT

IS THERE A *good kind* OF SADNESS?

IS IT CAUSED BY A *deeper love?*

CARE PACKAGES

Tangible gifts are a meaningful way to connect and send love from home.

Ideas:

- Send enough to share.

- Print or photocopy past and future calendar pages to share what I've been up to and what is coming up.

- Keep a box or envelope on the table, add to it each day, and mail it at the end of the week.

- Encourage our children to contribute ideas and items.

- Encourage members of our extended family to send care packages, too. Grandma can be in charge of books and Uncle Joe can take care of hygiene products.

- Keep it simple. A care package doesn't have to be expensive to be appreciated. I can be creative.

- Include a surprise in each package: a practical joke, homemade cookies.

- Mix it up between favorite items and new ones.

- Include items that represent the two of us: pictures of a favorite vacation, a piece of clothing that smells like me or like home.

- Send theme packages based on holidays, sports, seasons, superheroes, movies, or books.

- Send small travel games.

I AM

grateful

I HAVE SOMEONE

IN MY LIFE

I LOVE ENOUGH TO

miss so much

OUR LIFE

IS A

story

THIS

deployment

WON'T BE AN EMPTY

CHAPTER

COMMUNICATION

When we are far apart, our words matter more than ever. It's important to consider what needs to be said and the right time to say it.

I will:

- Appreciate the effort it takes to make a phone call from a deployed location.

- Try to see events and situations from other perspectives.

- Make time in every communication to express love.

- Think through what I want to say before I say it.

- Use "I" statements. (*"I feel angry when …"* instead of *"You make me angry when …"*)

- Be eager to share.

- Be ready to listen, even when I don't understand.

- Talk about one issue at a time.

- Avoid sarcasm, which can be misunderstood when communicating over distance.

- Accept apologies.

- Realize we won't always feel the same way, and that's okay.

- Understand that we might not be able to communicate in real time as often as I would like.

- Keep a list of topics to discuss or questions to ask the next time we talk.

INSTEAD OF

searching

FOR THE REASON

IT HAPPENED

create

THE REASON

IT MATTERS

REACHING OUT

Making new friends and helping others can be healing and provide needed support during deployment. There are many ways to connect, to help, and to allow others to help me.

I can:

- ~ Join a support group in person or online with other people who are going through a deployment.

- ~ Support other military families. I have something to offer others.

- ~ Help people in my community by volunteering for the Red Cross, USO, or local schools.

- ~ Connect with my family and others at my place of worship, or work, book club, or a fitness class.

- ~ Let my neighbors and coworkers know if I need help. People will support me if they know a little about what is going on in my life.

- ~ Ask someone I trust to coordinate offers of help for me or our family when I need it. I'll give that person a list of ways to help, and he or she can suggest tasks to those who offer help.

One step
AT A TIME
IS STILL MOVING
forward

MANAGING STRESS

Even good changes in life cause stress. I can manage my stress during deployment. The important thing is to find something that works for me and to do it consistently.

I can:

- Exercise: run, walk, swim, bike, try something new.

- Pray or meditate.

- Work on a puzzle. Play cards.

- Listen to quiet music or dance music. Choose the mood!

- Take five or ten deep breaths.

- Count to ten before reacting.

- Squeeze a stress ball.

- Ask for help. Offer help. Learn to say no.

- Write a list of things I am thankful for.

- Drink lots of water.

- Eat well.

- Sleep.

- Punch a pillow.

- Keep a notebook by my bed to jot down thoughts.

- Take a hot bath or shower.

- Minimize time on electronic devices.

- Do something creative: write, scrapbook, paint, draw, sew.

- Plant a garden.

114

- Start a new hobby.

- Strive for progress, not perfection.

- Get a facial, massage, pedicure, or manicure.

- Remember this deployment is a temporary situation.

- Limit alcohol consumption.

- Smell something nice.

- Get a babysitter.

- Bake.

- Order takeout.

- Read a good book. Join a book club—in person or online.

- Eliminate repetitive news. Don't listen to unofficial sources.

- Sit by the ocean or go to the park.

- Do random—or planned—acts of kindness.

- Confide in someone.

- Be honest with myself.

- Befriend someone who needs a friend. Volunteer. Help.

- Make time for myself every day.

- Cry. Laugh. Feel.

HANDLING FEAR

Deployments can be a source of fear and worry. I may not be able to avoid those, but there are actions I can take to manage them.

I can:

- Write down my fears. Sometimes just getting them out diminishes them.

- Allow myself only one worry or sad time per week.

- Share my fears with a friend. Avoid being alone when I'm afraid or worried.

- Find out everything I can about the thing I'm afraid of. A lack of information contributes to fear.

- Have a plan to calm my nerves and allow me to stop worrying. If I can't stop thinking about worst case scenarios, I will think them through and develop a plan for how I would deal with them.

- Buy or make a prayer or wish box. Put my concerns inside and shut the lid.

- Let go of fears I have no control over.

- Talk to a professional when I need to.

STRIVING IS
AS IMPORTANT AS
accomplishing
I WON'T LET
FEAR OF FAILURE
STOP ME FROM
trying

MAKING DECISIONS

While we are apart, we might not always be able to talk through decisions together. Sometimes, I will have to make important decisions on my own.

I can:

~ Make a list of pros and cons.

~ Think about why I want to say yes or no.

~ Consider which outcome aligns with values important to both of us.

~ Give myself an appropriate amount of time to make a good decision.

~ Allow myself time to think first, instead of making spontaneous decisions or commitments. Use a go-to phrase like, *"I will let you know by tomorrow,"* or *"I will check my calendar and get back to you."*

~ Write down what I think my decision should be, then put it away for a time. How do I feel about the decision later? A little distance may lend a new perspective.

~ Let strong feelings of sadness, anger, or loneliness pass before making a decision.

~ For financial decisions, make every effort to stick to the deployment budget and guidelines we chose together.

~ Forgive myself for decisions I regret. Give myself credit when my intentions were good.

~ Remember that doing my best is all I can do.

SOMETIMES THE

strongest

THING I CAN DO

IS BE

vulnerable

FAMILY ACTIVITIES

Deployments are hard on children, too, but there are still lots of ways to make this time fun and memorable.

I can:

- Let kids be kids. Don't assign them too many grownup roles, which can be confusing and increase anxiety.

- Let children take turns selecting an activity for family fun night.

- Take turns planning dinners for each other.

- Create a scrapbook or a family newsletter.

- Make a video of our family during deployment. Plan, edit, and produce it like a movie.

- Hold a tournament of board games.

- Draw a circle on a map enclosing an eighty-mile radius from home. Explore a new place within that circle each weekend.

- Dance. Teach each other new dance moves.

- Build a tent in the living room and sleep in it.

- Leave love notes for the kids: in school lunches, on the shower wall using soap, in shoes, or under their pillows.

- Give them grace. Children experience all the emotions of deployment with less ability to understand or control them.

- Remember that my role is to keep my kids healthy and safe. I can't do everything, but I can focus on our priorities, be consistent, and provide a sense of stability.

~ Say *"I love you"* every day. Especially on the hardest days.

~ Model forgiveness. Model kindness.

~ Limit screen time on phones, tablets, and televisions. Limits are good for everybody. Work together to set guidelines and stick to them.

~ Volunteer together: Visit an animal shelter. Clean up a park. Walk for a cause.

~ Find creative ways to help kids keep their deployed parent visually present in their daily lives, such as a bedside photo, laminated photo inside a backpack pocket, or short video with a special message. Have fun including a life-size cardboard cutout of the deployed parent, photo-on-a-stick, or other visual representation in family photos, vacation memories, or holiday celebrations. Be creative and silly.

~ Remember that my stress can affect my children, too. Managing my own stress is a way to care for my children as well as myself.

DEPLOYMENT

Returning home

Homecoming is on the horizon!

Time to get ready! Before homecoming I want to...

As I prepare for homecoming ...

I look forward to ... I wish ... I hope ... I worry about ... I wonder ...

➤ *I wish we had ...* ➤ *I am so glad ...* ➤ *special memories of this time apart ...* ◄

As homecoming day draws near, I feel ...

Sexy → *Vulnerable* → *Appreciated* → *Emotional* → *Stressed* → *Restless* → *Calm*

Ecstatic → *Bummed* → *Overjoyed* → *Hesitant* → *Patient* → *Tender* → *Blessed*

→ *Forgiving* → *Irritable* → *Delighted* → *Insecure* → *Proud* → *Elated* → *Bashful* → *Inspired*

HOMECOMING *and* REUNION

Deployment brings change and growth. No matter how much I hope life will go back to the way it was before the deployment, I realize we have grown through this experience and it may take time to reconnect.

I will:

- Look forward to homecoming with excitement!

- Plan for a readjustment period. We will be happy to be together again, but we will also need time to adjust and acclimate to life together at home.

- Remember that we have each gone through very meaningful—but very different—experiences while we were apart.

- Think about how our responsibilities have shifted, how my expectations have changed, and the challenges we've overcome. These change the dynamics of any relationship.

- Be prepared to get reacquainted slowly and understand that each of us will adapt back to life together in different ways.

- Remind myself of the reasons we love each other and what makes this journey worthwhile.

Homecoming day ...

❧ when, where ... ❧ who was there ... ❧ what I was wearing ... ❧ the waiting ...
❧ the moment we first saw each other ... ❧ what we said to each other ... ❧

Our first days together again ...

Now that we are together again, I feel ...

Flirtatious ❧ Competitive ❧ Appreciated ❧ Wonderful ❧ Stressed ❧ Embarrassed ❧ Forgiving ❧ Infuriated ❧ Enchanted ❧ Insecure ❧ Wanted ❧ Different ❧ Discouraged 167 ❧ Tired ❧ Sympathetic ❧ Relieved ❧ Hurt ❧ Affectionate ❧ Kind ❧ Peaceful ❧

Looking forward

The impact of this deployment on me ...

❧ *how I've grown personally ...* ❧ *ways my perspective has changed ...* ❧ *my health ...*
❧ *my other relationships ...* ❧ *Am I a better friend, parent, partner? ...* ❧

How this deployment has changed our relationship ...

❧ *our communication ...* ❧ *perspective ...* ❧ *new things we've learned about each other ...*
❧ *ways we've grown closer ...* ❧ *new feelings we've discovered ...* ☙

171

Lessons I've learned during this deployment ...

➤ what I'd do differently or keep the same ... ➤ advice to myself for next time ... ➤

As I look forward to the future, I feel ….

Hopeful ❧ *Bored* ❧ *Challenged* ❧ *Adamant* ❧ *Energized* ❧ *Free* ❧ *Honored*

Bitter ❧ *Overjoyed* ❧ *Inspired* ❧ *Depressed* ❧ *Grieving* ❧ *Loved* ❧ *Faithful*

❧ *Odd* ❧ *Capable* ❧ *Enthusiastic* ❧ *Pleased* ❧ *Impressed* ❧ *Planful* ❧ *Flustered* ❧ *Silly*

This experience
IS JUST ONE
ON OUR
life's adventure
TOGETHER

Memories and milestones

Making note of important moments—big or small—during this deployment can help me remember and share: accomplishments, milestones, special connections, sweet memories ...

DATE: DESCRIPTION:

_____   _____
          _____
          _____

_____   _____
          _____
          _____

_____   _____
          _____
          _____

_____   _____
          _____
          _____

_____   _____
          _____
          _____

_____   _____
          _____
          _____

_____   _____
          _____

DATE: DESCRIPTION:

_____ _____
_____
_____

_____ _____
_____
_____

_____ _____
_____
_____

_____ _____
_____
_____

_____ _____
_____
_____

_____ _____
_____
_____

_____ _____
_____
_____

DATE: DESCRIPTION:

_____

_____

_____

_____

_____

_____

_____

I AM

grateful

FOR EACH MOMENT:

smiles, tears, hopes, fears

BECAUSE THESE MOMENTS

MADE ME

who I am

TODAY

DATE: DESCRIPTION:

DATE: DESCRIPTION:

_____   _____
           _____
           _____
           _____

_____   _____
           _____
           _____
           _____

_____   _____
           _____
           _____
           _____

_____   _____
           _____
           _____
           _____

_____   _____
           _____
           _____
           _____

_____   _____
           _____
           _____
           _____

_____   _____
           _____
           _____

_____   _____
           _____
           _____

DATE: DESCRIPTION:

_____   _____

DATE: DESCRIPTION:

DATE: DESCRIPTION:

DATE: DESCRIPTION:

_____

_____

_____

_____

_____

_____

_____

DATE: DESCRIPTION:

DATE: DESCRIPTION:

_____   _____
                     _____
                     _____

_____   _____
                     _____
                     _____

_____   _____
                     _____
                     _____

_____   _____
                     _____
                     _____

_____   _____
                     _____
                     _____

_____   _____
                     _____
                     _____

_____   _____
                     _____
                     _____

_____   _____